# RAISING THEM

# RIGHT

## *A Saint's Advice on Raising Children*

### BY THEOPHAN THE RECLUSE

Foreword by Peter E. Gillquist

© 1989 Conciliar Press

Ben Lomond, California

RAISING THEM RIGHT
Copyright © 1989 Conciliar Press
Second Printing 1995
Ben Lomond, California

ISBN 0-9622713-0-6
All Rights Reserved
Library of Congress Catalog Card Number: 89-061280

Originally printed under the title *The Path to Salvation*
by Eastern Orthodox Press, Etna, California

# Contents

# Foreword

Ever so rarely, you come upon a book from the past—decades old, centuries old, or even something from the pre-Christian era—that you sense is timeless. Though seasoned by age its message seems more up to date than this morning's paper.

*Proverbs*, from the Old Testament, would be such a book. So too, *The Ladder of Divine Ascent* from the sixth century, written by Saint John Climacus. More modernly, many of the writings of C. S. Lewis seem to carry a similar sense of universal permanence.

Now, I feel we have found another.

Many years ago, a monk named Theophan—whom we know best by his writings on prayer and spiritual warfare—wrote a classic book entitled *The Path to Salvation*. This book is a summation of Saint Theophan's teachings on spirituality and Christian development. And it includes some incredible material on how to raise children to be followers of our Lord Jesus Christ and keepers of the flame within His Holy Church. Through the efforts of Lawrence Williams, a translation of this portion of *The Path to Salvation* was published in book form in the early 1980's. Recently, Mr. Williams came to Conciliar Press and made the volume available for updating and republication. We have since added our own chapter breaks, subheads, and introductory material. And we have entitled the work *Raising Them Right*.

Two things struck me as I read this material. First, this is *classic* Orthodox wisdom and instruction on how to raise children for Christ. Secondly, and I'm not sure we can answer this, how can a monastic recluse know this much about families and children?

I believe that *Raising Them Right* is prophetic for our time. Its message is a fresh breath of hope and promise for parents and pastors alike. May it be used to shape countless thousands of our children—and us adults—more fully into the image and likeness of God.

Fr. Peter E. Gillquist
Santa Barbara, California

## Life of Saint Theophan the Recluse

Theophan the Recluse (1815-94) was born at Chernavsk, near Orlov, in the central Russian province of Viatka. His given name was George Vasilyevich Govorov. His father was a parish priest, and his mother was kindly and devout. After attending clerical school, he was sent to a seminary to be trained for the priesthood. He was a brilliant student finishing at the top of his class. Even at this period of life, his teachers described him as "disposed to solitude, gentle, and silent." After seminary, he studied for four years at the Theological Academy of Kiev. Here, he visited the caves of the Kievo-Pechersk Lavra, (the cradle of Russian monasticism), and gained lasting impressions of monastic life.

After graduation from the Academy, Theophan took monastic vows and was ordained to the priesthood. His great academic skills caused him to advance rapidly. First, in 1841, he became headmaster of the Kiev Theological school. Later he became a professor in the Saint Petersburg Ecclesiastical Academy. Finally he was made rector of Olenetz Seminary in 1855, and of Saint Petersburg Academy in 1857.

In 1847 Theophan was sent to serve for seven years in Palestine, Constantinople, and the Near East as a member of the Orthodox Mission in the Holy Land. During this time he learned Greek and, through reading the many spiritual books he found in the Near East libraries, he became better acquainted with the Fathers. The later writings of Theophan draw heavily from this patristic background.

On June 1, 1859, Theophan was consecrated bishop. He served four years in the See of Tambov, and then was transferred to the diocese of Vladimir. Two years after his own consecration, Saint Tikhon of Zadonsk was canonized. From his childhood Bishop Theophan had held a special love for Saint Tikhon, and from this time on he consciously and zealously began to imitate Saint Tikhon's example of asceticism.

Although a kindly bishop, a good administrator, and a strong preacher, Bishop Theophan grew increasingly weary of public office. He longed to lead a life of prayer and seclusion. In 1866 he resigned from his active work of diocesan administration and, after preaching his final message to an enormous crowd at the Cathedral of Vladimir, retired to a remote monastery hidden in the great forests at Vyshen. Here he was to remain in seclusion until his death twenty-eight years later.

Theophan was appointed abbot of the monastery, and for the first six years of his life there, took an active part in the monastic services. Beginning in 1872, however, Theophan became a recluse. He remained strictly secluded, never going outside his cell, seeing no one but his confessor and the superior of his monastery. His was a life of complete solitude. As a recluse for the rest of his life, Theophan devoted himself to prayer and asceticism, to correspondence, and to literary work.

His personal discipline was astounding. His daily diet consisted of nothing more than the barest essentials—tea, a few pieces of bread, and during non-fast periods a bit of milk and one or two eggs—just enough to keep his health. His cell had two barely furnished rooms, including a small domestic chapel with just the basic, necessary liturgical items. During the later years of his life he celebrated the Divine Liturgy daily in his own chapel, by himself, without a server. He continually prayed the Jesus Prayer, and constantly strove to perfect in himself the practice of "prayer of the mind in the heart."

In addition to his own ascetical labors, he spent hours every day corresponding with people from all over Russia. He received from twenty to forty letters per day, and faithfully answered them all. Though he never met face to face with the people with whom he corresponded, he gave insightful direction to his spiritual children through his letters. He also gained from them an understanding of contemporary problems otherwise denied to him by his secluded lifestyle. His insight into contemporary situations and life was prophetic in nature. Much of this correspondence has been saved and compiled, and is partially published in ten volumes. The wonderful spiritual anthology *The Art of Prayer* [1] draws heavily from this correspondence.

Theophan brought with him into his seclusion a library of spiritual literature, ranging from the early Fathers to contemporary theology and philosophy. The thoughts and spirit of the

---

[1] *The Art of Prayer: An Orthodox Anthology*; Compiled by Igumen Chariton of Valamo; Translated by E. Kadloubovsky and E. M. Palmer; Edited and with an introduction by Timothy Ware. London, Faber and Faber, 1966.

Fathers filled his counsels and writings. He spent much time translating various spiritual works into Russian to make them accessable to the Russian people. Not only a translator, he wrote many ascetical works of his own. Especially important are his teachings on the use of the Jesus Prayer, and prayer of the heart. He wrote theological and catechetical material on a simple, basic level that would be understandable to the less educated. He also wrote commentaries on the Epistles of Saint Paul.

For years the faithful of Russia (and others around the world as his written works became known) have recognized in Theophan a truly spirit-filled man and guiding light in the area of personal spirituality. Just recently, however, he has been officially recognized for his sanctity of life and given a place of special honor in the Church. In an official act of the local council of the Russian Orthodox Church on June 6, 1988, Bishop Theophan the Recluse, along with eight other Russian Orthodox faithful, was officially canonized.

May Saint Theophan's life be an example to us all!

*Text Translated from the Russian
by Hieromonk Seraphim Rose*

# Chapter One
## The Christian Adult

It is possible to describe the feelings and inclinations which a Christian must have, but this is very far from being all that is demanded for the ordering of one's salvation. The important thing for us is a real life in the spirit of Christ. But just touch on this, and how many perplexities are uncovered, how many guideposts are necessary, as a result, almost at every step!

True, one may know man's final goal: communion with God. And one may describe the path to it: faith, and walking in the commandments, with the aid of Divine grace. One need only say in addition: here is the path—start walking!

This is easily said, but how to do it? For the most part the very desire to walk is lacking. The soul, attracted by some passion or other, stubbornly repulses every compelling force and every call; the eyes turn away from God and do not want to look at Him. The law of Christ is not to one's liking; there is no disposition even to listen to it.

One may ask, how does one reach the point where the desire is born to walk toward God on the path of Christ? What does one do so that the law will imprint itself on the heart, and man, acting according to this law, will act as if from himself, unconstrained, so that this law will not lie on him, but will as it were proceed from him?

But suppose someone has turned toward God, suppose he has

7

come to love His law. Is the very going toward God, the very walking on the path of Christ's law, already necessary and will it be successful merely because we desire it to be? No. Besides the desire, one must also have the strength and knowledge to act; one must have active wisdom.

Whoever enters on the true path of pleasing God, or whoever begins with the aid of grace to strive toward God on the path of Christ's law, will inevitably be threatened by the danger of losing his way at the crossroads, of going astray and perishing, imagining himself saved. These crossroads are unavoidable because of the sinful inclinations and disorder of one's faculties which are capable of presenting things in a false light—to deceive and destroy a man.

To this is joined the flattery of Satan, who is reluctant to be separated from his victims and, when someone from his domain goes to the light of Christ, pursues him and sets every manner of net in order to catch him again—and quite often he indeed catches him.

Consequently it is necessary for someone who already has the desire to walk on the indicated path to the Lord to be shown in addition all the deviations that are possible on this path, so that the traveller may be warned in advance about this, may see the dangers that are to be encountered, and may know how to avoid them.

These general considerations —unavoidable to all on the path of salvation—render indispensable certain guiding rules of the Christian life. By these guiding rules it may be determined how to attain to the saving desire for communion with God and the zeal to remain in it, and how to reach God without misfortune amidst all the crossroads that may be met on this path at every step—in other words, how to begin to live the Christian life and how, having begun, to perfect oneself in it.

The sowing and development of the Christian life are different in essence from the sowing and development of natural life, owing to the special character of the Christian life and its relation to our nature. A man is not born a Christian, but becomes such after birth. The seed of Christ falls on the soil of a heart that is already beating.

But since the naturally-born man is injured and opposed by the demand of Christianity—while in a plant, for example, the beginning of life is the stirring of a sprout in the seed, an awakening of as it were dormant powers—the beginning of a true Christian life in a man is a kind of recreation, an endowing of new powers, of new life.

Further, suppose that Christianity is received as a law, the resolution is made to live a Christian life; this seed of life (this resolution) is not surrounded in a man by elements favorable to him. Besides this, the whole man—his body and soul—remain unadapted to the new life, unsubmissive to the yoke of Christ. Therefore from this moment begins in a man a labor of sweat, a labor to educate his whole self, all his faculties, according to the Christian standard.

This is why, while growth in plants, for example, is a gradual development of faculties—easy, unconstrained—in a Christian it is a battle with oneself involving much labor, intense and sorrowful, and he must dispose his faculties for something for which they have no inclination. Like a soldier, he must take every step of land, even his own, from his enemies by means of warfare, with the double-edged sword of forcing himself and opposing himself.

Finally, after long labors and exertions, the Christian principles appear victorious, reigning without opposition; they penetrate the whole composition of human nature, dislodging from it demands and inclinations hostile to themselves, and place it in a state of passionlessness and purity, making it worthy of the blessedness of the pure in heart—to see God in themselves in sincerest communion with Him.

Such is the place in us of the Christian life. This life has three stages which may be called:

1) Turning to God;
2) Purification or self-amendment;
3) Sanctification.

In the first stage a man turns from darkness to light, from the domain of Satan to God; in the second, he cleanses the chamber of his heart from every impurity, in order to receive Christ the Lord Who is coming to him; in the third, the Lord comes, takes up His abode in his heart, and communes with him. This is the state of blessed communion with God—the goal of all labors and ascetic endeavors.

## HOW DOES THE CHRISTIAN LIFE BEGIN IN US?

We must make clear for ourselves when and how the Christian life truly begins in order to see whether we have within ourselves the beginning of this life. If we do not have it, we must learn how to begin it, in so far as this depends upon us.

It is not yet a decisive sign of true life in Christ if one calls himself a Christian and belongs to the Church of Christ. "Not everyone who says to Me, 'Lord, Lord,' shall enter the kingdom of heaven" (Matthew 7:21). "For they are not all Israel who are of Israel" (Romans 9:6). One can be counted as a Christian and not be a Christian. This everyone knows.

There is a moment, and a very noticeable moment, which sharply is marked out in the course of our life, when a person begins to live in a Christian way. This is the moment when there begins to be present in him the distinctive characteristics of Christian life. Christian life is zeal, and the strength to remain in communion with God by means of an active fulfillment of His holy will, according to our faith in our Lord Jesus Christ, and with the help of the grace of God, to the glory of His most holy name.

The essence of Christian life consists in communion with

10

God, in Christ Jesus our Lord—in a communion with God which in the beginning is usually hidden not only from others, but also from oneself. The testimony of this life that is visible or can be felt within us is the ardor of active zeal to please God alone in a Christian manner, with total self-sacrifice and hatred of everything which is opposed to this. And so, when this ardor of zeal begins, Christian life has its beginning. And the person in whom this ardor is constantly active is one who is living in a Christian way.

Here we will have to stop and pay more attention to this distinctive characteristic.

"I came to send fire on the earth," the Saviour said, "and how I wish it were already kindled!" (Luke 12:49). He is speaking here of Christian life, and He says this because the visible witness of it is the zeal for the pleasing of God which is in the heart by the Spirit of God. This is like fire because, just as fire devours the material which it takes hold of, so also does zeal for the life in Christ devour the soul which receives it. And just as during the time of a fire the flame takes hold of the whole building, so also the fire of zeal, once it is received, embraces and fills the whole being of a man.

In another place the Lord says, "Everyone will be seasoned with fire" (Mark 9:49). This also is an indication of the fire of the spirit which in its zeal penetrates our whole being. Just as salt, penetrating decomposable matter, preserves it from decomposition, so also the spirit of zeal, penetrating our whole being, banishes the sin which corrupts our nature both in soul and body; it banishes it even from the least of the places where it has settled in us, and thus it saves us from moral vice and corruption.

The Apostle Paul commands, "Do not quench the Spirit" (I Thessalonians 5:19), and "not lagging in diligence, [be] fervent in spirit, serving the Lord" (Romans 12:11). He commands this to all Christians so that we might remember that the fervor of the spirit, or unslothful striving, is an inseparable attribute of Christian life.

In another place he speaks of himself thus: "Forgetting those things which are behind and reaching forward to those things which are ahead, I press on toward the goal for the prize of the upward call of God in Christ Jesus" (Philippians 3:13-14). And to others he says, "Run in such a way that you may obtain it" (I Corinthians 9:24).

This means that in Christian life the result of the fervor of zeal is a certain quickness and liveliness of spirit, with which people undertake God-pleasing works, trampling upon oneself and willingly offering as a sacrifice to God every kind of labor, without sparing oneself.

Having a firm basis in such an understanding, one may easily conclude that a cold fulfillment of the rules of the Church—just like routine in business, which is established by our calculating mind, or like correct and dignified behavior and honesty in conduct—these are not decisive indicators that the true Christian life is present in us.

All this is good, but as long as it does not bear in itself the spirit of life in Christ Jesus, it has no value at all before God. Such things would then be like soul-less statues. Good clocks also work correctly; but who will say that there is life in them? It is the same thing here. "I know your works, that you have a name that you are alive, but you are dead" (Revelation 3:1).

This good order in one's conduct more than anything else can lead one into deception. Its true significance depends upon one's inward disposition, where it is possible that there are significant deviations from real righteousness in one's righteous deeds.

Thus, while refraining outwardly from sinful deeds, one may have an attraction for them or a delight from them in one's heart; so also, doing righteous deeds outwardly, one's heart may not be in them. Only true zeal both wishes to do good in all fulness and purity, and persecutes sin in its smallest forms. It seeks the good

12

as its daily bread, and it fights with sin as with a mortal enemy. An enemy hates an enemy not only personally, but he hates also relatives and friends of this enemy, and even his belongings, his favorite color, and in general anything that might remind one of him. So also, true zeal to please God persecutes sin in its smallest reminders or marks, for it is zealous for perfect purity. If this is not present, how much impurity can hide in the heart!

## ZEAL

And what success can one expect when there is no enthusiastic zeal for a Christian pleasing of God? If there is something that involves no labor, one is ready to do it; but as soon as one is required to do a little extra labor, or some kind of self-sacrifice, immediately one refuses, because one is unable to accomplish it oneself. For then there will be nothing to rely on that can move one to good deeds: self-pity will undermine all the foundations. And if any other motive besides the one mentioned becomes involved, it will make the good deed into a bad deed.

The spies under Moses spared themselves because they were afraid. The martyrs willingly went to death because they were kindled by an inward fire. A true zealot does not do only what is according to the law, but also what has been advised, following every good suggestion that has been secretly imprinted on the soul; he does not only what has been given, but he is also an acquirer of good things; he is entirely concerned with the one good thing which is solid, true, and eternal.

Saint John Chrysostom says: "Everywhere we must have fervor and much fire of the soul, prepared to be armed against death itself. For otherwise it is impossible to receive the kingdom" (Homily 31 on the Acts).

The work of piety and communion with God is a work of much labor and much pain, especially in the beginning. Where can we find the power to undertake all these labors? With the help of

God's grace, we can find it in heartfelt zeal.

A merchant, a soldier, a judge, or a scholar has work which is full of cares and difficulties. How do they sustain themselves in the midst of their labors? By enthusiasm and love for their work. And one cannot sustain oneself by anything else on the path of piety either. Without this we will be serving God in a state of sluggishness, boredom, and lack of interest. An animal like the sloth also moves, but with difficulty, while for the swift gazelle or the nimble squirrel movement and getting about are a delight. Zealous pleasing of God is the path to God which is full of consolation and gives wings to the spirit. Without it one can ruin everything.

One must do everything for the glory of God in defiance of the sin which dwells in us. Without this we will do everything only out of habit, because it seems "proper," because this is the way it has always been done, or the way others do it. We must do all we can, otherwise we will do some things and neglect others, and this without any contrition or even knowledge of what we have omitted. We must do everything with heedfulness and care, as our chief task, otherwise we will do everything just as it comes.

And so, it is clear that without zeal a Christian is a poor Christian. He is drowsy, feeble, lifeless, neither hot nor cold—and this kind of life is not life at all. Knowing this, let us strive to manifest ourselves as true zealots of good deeds, so that we might truly be pleasing to God, having neither stain nor spot, nor any of these things.

Therefore, a true witness of Christian life is the fire of active zeal for the pleasing of God. Now the question arises, how is this fire ignited? Who produces it?

Such zeal is produced by the action of grace. However, it does not occur without the participation of our free will. Christian life is not natural life. This should be the way it begins or is first aroused: as in a seed, growth is aroused when moisture and warmth penetrate to the sprout which is hidden within, and through these the all-restoring power of life comes; so also in us, the Divine life is aroused when the Spirit of God penetrates into the heart and places there the beginning of life according to the Spirit, and cleanses and gathers into one the darkened and broken features of the image of God.

A desire and free seeking are aroused (by an action from without); then grace descends (through the Mysteries) and, uniting with our freedom, produces a mighty zeal. But let no one think that he himself can give birth to such a power of life; one must pray for this and be ready to receive it. The fire of zeal with power—this is the grace of the Lord. The Spirit of God, descending into the heart, begins to act in it with a zeal that is both devouring and all-active.

To some the thought arises: does there need to be this action of grace? Can we ourselves really not do good deeds? After all, we have done this or that good deed, and, if we live longer, we will do some more. Perhaps it is a rare person who does not ask this question. Others say that of ourselves we can do nothing good. But here the question is not only of separate good deeds, but of giving rebirth to our whole life, to a new life, to life in its entirety— to such a life as can lead one to salvation.

As a matter of fact, it is not difficult to do something which is even quite good, as the pagans also did. But let someone intentionally define a course for himself of a continuous doing of good, and define the order of it according to what is indicated in the word of God—and this not for one month or for a year, but for one's whole life—and place as a rule to remain in this order unwaveringly; and then, when he will remain faithful to this, let him boast of his own power. But without this it is better to close one's mouth.

How many cases there have been in the past and in the present of a self-trusting beginning and building of a Christian life! And

15

they have all ended and continue to end in nothing.

A man builds a little in his new order of life—and then throws it away. And how can it be otherwise? There is no strength. It is characteristic only of the eternal power of God to support us unchanging in our disposition in the midst of the unceasing waves of temporal changes. Therefore one must be filled abundantly with this power; one must ask for it and receive it in order—and it will raise us up and draw us out of the great agitation of temporal life.

# Chapter Two
## Baptism: The Adult and the Child

Let us turn now to experience and see when it is that such thoughts of self-satisfaction come.

When a man is in a calm condition, when nothing is disturbing him, nothing is deceiving him or leading him into sin—then he is ready for every kind of holy and pure life. But as soon as the movement of a passion or a temptation comes, where are all the promises? Does a man not often say to himself as he leads an unrestrained life, "Now I will no longer do this"? But once the passions again become hungry, a new impulse arises, and again he finds himself in sins.

### THE MIRE: TRUSTING IN ONESELF

It is all well and good to reflect on the bearing of offenses when everything is going according to our will, and not against our self-love. In fact, here it would be rather strange to have a feeling of offense or anger such as others might give themselves over to. But just find yourself in the opposite condition, and then a single glance—not even a word—will make you beside yourself!

Thus you may well dream, trusting in yourself, about leading a Christian life without any help from above—as long as your soul is calm. But when the evil that lies in the depths of the heart is roused up like dust by the wind, then in your own experience you will find the condemnation of your own presumption.

When thought after thought, desire after desire—one worse than the other—begin to disturb the soul, then everyone forgets about himself and involuntarily cries out with the prophet: "The waters have come up to my neck. I sink in deep mire, where there is no standing. I have come into the deep waters, where the floods overflow me" (Psalm 69: 1-2). "Save now, I pray, O Lord; O Lord, I pray, send now prosperity" (Psalm 118:25).

And often it happens in this way: someone dreams of remaining in the good, trusting in himself. But a face or a thing comes to the imagination, desire is born, passion is aroused: a man is attracted and falls. After this one need only look at oneself and say: How bad that was! But then an opportunity for distraction comes, and again one is ready to forget oneself.

Again, someone has offended you, a battle begins, there are reproaches and judgment. Some unjust but convenient way of looking at it presents itself to your mind, and you seize it. You belittle someone, spread the tale to others, confuse someone else—and all this after you were boasting of the possibility of leading a holy life by yourself, without special help from above. Where was your strength then? "The spirit indeed is willing, but the flesh is weak" (Matthew 26:41). You see good and do evil: "For the good that I will to do, I do not do; but the evil I will not to do, that I practice" (Romans 7:19). We are in captivity. Redeem us, O Lord!

One of the first tricks of the enemy against us is the idea of trusting in oneself: that is, if not renouncing, then at least not feeling the need for the help of grace. The enemy as it were says: "Do not go to the light where they wish to give you some kind of new powers. You are good just the way you are!" And a man gives himself over to repose. But in the meantime the enemy is throwing a rock (some kind of unpleasantness) at one; others he is leading into a slippery place (the deception of the passions); for yet others he is strewing with flowers a closed noose (deceptively good conditions). Without looking around, a man strives to go further and further, and does not guess that he is falling down lower and lower until finally he goes to the very depths of evil, to the threshold of hell itself. Should one not in such a case cry out to him as to the first Adam: "Man, where are you? Where have you gone?" This very cry is the action of grace, which compels a sinner for the first time to look about himself.

Therefore, if you desire to begin to live in a Christian way, seek grace. The minute when grace descends and joins itself to your will is the minute when the Christian life is born in you— powerful, firm, and greatly fruitful.

Where can one obtain and how can one receive the grace which gives the beginning of life? The acquisition of grace and the sanctification of our nature by its means is performed in the Mysteries. Here we offer of God's action, or present to God our own worthless nature; and He, by His action, transforms it. It was pleasing to God, in order to strike down our proud mind, to hide His power at the very beginning of true life beneath the covering of simple materiality. How this happens we do not understand, but the experience of all Christianity testifies that it does not happen otherwise.

The Mysteries which primarily refer to the beginning of the Christian life are baptism and repentance. Therefore, the rules concerning the beginning of life in a true Christian way are set forth first under the heading of baptism, and then under repentance.

## HOW THE CHRISTIAN LIFE BEGINS
## IN THE SACRAMENT OF BAPTISM

Baptism is the first Mystery (Sacrament) in Christianity; it makes a Christian man worthy to be vouchsafed the gifts of grace through other Mysteries also. Without it one cannot enter into the Christian world and become a member of the Church.

The Pre-eternal Wisdom has made a house for Himself upon earth, and the door leading into this house is the Mystery of baptism. By this door not only do people enter into the house of God, but at this door also they are clothed in a garment worthy of it, they receive a new name and a sign which is impressed upon the whole being of the one being baptized, by means of which, later, both heavenly and earthly beings recognize and distinguish them.

"If anyone is in Christ, he is a new creation," teaches the Apostle (II Corinthians 5:17). This new creation becomes a Christian in baptism. From the font a man comes out not at all the way he went in. As light is to darkness, as life is to death, so is a baptized man opposed to one who is unbaptized.

Conceived in iniquities and born in sins, a man before baptism bears in himself all the poison of sin, with all the weight of its consequences. He is in a condition of God's disfavor, and is by nature a child of wrath. He is ruined, disordered in himself with relation to his parts and powers which are directed primarily towards the multiplication of sin. He is in subjection to the influence of Satan, who acts in him with power by reason of the sin which dwells in him. As a result of all this, after death he is unfailingly the child of hell, where he must be tormented together with its prince and his helpers and servants.

Baptism delivers us from all these evils. It takes away the curse by the power of the Cross of Christ and returns the blessing. Those who are baptized are the children of God, as the Lord Himself has given them the right to be: "And if children, then heirs—heirs of God and joint-heirs with Christ" (Romans 8:17).

The Kingdom of Heaven belongs to the baptized person already by virtue of his baptism. He is taken away from the dominion of Satan, who now loses authority over him and the power to act arbitrarily in him. By entrance into the Church—the house of refuge—Satan is denied access to the newly baptized one. He finds himself here as in a safe enclosure.

20

All these are spiritually outward privileges and gifts. But what happens inwardly? The healing of the affliction and injury of sin. The power of grace penetrates within and restores here the Divine order in all its beauty. It treats the disorder in the structure and relationship of the powers and parts, as well as changing the chief orientation from oneself to God—to pleasing God and increasing one's good deeds.

Therefore, baptism is a rebirth or a new birth which puts a man in a renewed condition. The Apostle Paul compares all the baptized with the resurrected Saviour, giving us to understand that they also have the same bright nature in their renewal as was possessed by the human nature of the Lord Jesus through His resurrection in glory (Romans 6:4).

And that the orientation of activity in a baptized person is changed may be seen in the words of the same Apostle, who says in another place that they already "should live no longer for themselves, but for Him Who died for them and rose again" (II Corinthians 5:15). "For the death that He died, He died to sin once for all; but the life that He lives, He lives to God" (Romans 6:10). "We were buried with Him through baptism into death" (Romans 6:4); and: "Our old man was crucified with Him, that the body of sin might be done away with, that we should no longer be slaves of sin" (Romans 6:6).

And so, the whole activity of a person by the power of baptism is turned away from oneself and sin, and towards God and righteousness.

Remarkable are the words of the Apostle: "That we should no longer be slaves of sin" (Romans 6:6), as well as his other words: "Sin shall not have dominion over you" (Romans 6:14). This gives us to understand that the power which, in our disordered, fallen nature, draws us towards sin, is not entirely exterminated in baptism, but is only placed in a condition in which it has no power over us, no dominion over us, and we do not serve it. But it is still

21

in us, it lives and acts, only not as a lord. The primacy from now on belongs to the grace of God and to the soul that consciously gives itself over to it.

Saint Diadoch, explaining the power of baptism, says that before baptism sin dwells in the heart and grace acts from outside, but after baptism, grace settles in the heart and sin attracts us from outside. It is banished from the heart as an enemy from a fortress, and it settles outside, in the parts of the body, from where it acts by means of attacks in a fragmented state. This is why there is a constant tempter, a seducer, but no longer a master: he disturbs and alarms, but does not command (*Philokalia*, Part 4).

And so, the new life is born in baptism!

Here our attention will be directed to how the Christian life begins through baptism in those who were baptized as children—just how this occurs. For here the beginning of Christian life is put in order in a special way which comes from the relationship of grace to freedom.

You already know that grace descends upon free desire and searching, and that only by the mutual cooperation of these two is there begun the new grace-given life which is in accordance both with grace and with the nature of the free person. The Lord gives grace freely. But He asks that a man seek it and receive it with desire, dedicating himself entirely to God.

The fulfillment of this condition in repentance and in the baptism of adults is clear. But how is it fulfilled in the baptism of infants? An infant does not have the use of reason and freedom; consequently, he cannot fulfill the condition for the beginning of Christian life on his own part—that is, the desire to dedicate himself to God. Nevertheless, this condition must absolutely be fulfilled. The particular way in which (Christian) life begins in the case of the baptism of infants depends on the means of fulfilling this condition.

## BAPTISM FOR INFANTS

Grace descends upon the soul of an infant and produces in it exactly the same result as if its freedom had participated in this, but only on the condition that in the future the infant, who was not then aware of himself and did not act personally, when he comes to awareness, will himself willingly dedicate himself to God, will receive out of his own desire the grace which has shown its activity in him, will be glad that it exists, will give thanks that this was done for him, and will confess that if, at the moment of his baptism, understanding and freedom had been given to him, he would not have acted otherwise than he did act and would not have wished otherwise.

For the sake of this future free dedication of himself to God and the coming together of freedom and grace, divine grace gives everything to the infant and even without him it produces everything in him that is natural for it to produce, with the promise that the essential desire and dedicating of himself to God will be performed without fail. This is the promise which the sponsors give when they declare to God before the Church that this infant, when he comes to awareness, will show precisely that use of freedom which is demanded for grace, taking upon themselves the obligation in very fact to bring to this state the infant for whom they are sponsors.

And thus through baptism the seed of life in Christ is placed in the infant and exists in him; but it is as though it did not exist: it acts as an educating power in him. Spiritual life, conceived by the grace of baptism in the infant, becomes the property of the man and is manifest in its complete form in accordance not only with grace, but also with the character of the rational creature from the time when he, coming to awareness, by his own free will dedicates himself to God and appropriates to himself the power of grace in himself by receiving it with desire, joy, and gratitude. Up to this time also, the true Christian life is active in him, but it is as if without his knowledge; it acts in him, but it is as if it is not yet his own. But from the minute of his awareness and choosing, it becomes his own, not by grace only but also by freedom.

Because of this more or less prolonged interval between baptism and the dedication of oneself to God, the beginning of Christian moral life through the grace of baptism in infants is broadened, so to speak, into an indefinite period of time, during which the infant matures and is formed into a Christian in the Holy Church in the midst of other Christians, as previously he had been formed bodily in the womb of his mother.

Stop, O reader, a little longer on this idea. It will be very necessary to us to define how parents, sponsors, and educators should behave with regard to the baptized infant who is entrusted to them by the Holy Church and the Lord.

It goes without saying that after the baptism of the infant a very important matter stands before the parents and the sponsors: how to lead the baptized one so that when he comes to awareness he might recognize the grace-given powers within himself and accept them with a joyful desire, together with the obligations and way of life which they demand. This places one face to face with the question of Christian upbringing, or the upbringing which is in accordance with the demands of the grace of baptism and has as its aim the preservation of this grace.

So that it might be clear how one must act with regard to a baptized infant with these aims in mind, one must recall the above-mentioned idea that grace overshadows the heart and dwells in it when there is in the heart a turning away from sin and a turning towards God. If this attitude is manifested in act, there are further given all the other gifts of grace and all the characteristics of one who is dwelling in grace: the favor of God, the co-inheritance with Christ, the dwelling outside the sphere of Satan, out of the danger of being condemned to hell. But as soon as this attitude of mind and heart decreases or is lost, immediately sin again begins to

24

possess the heart, and through sin the bonds of Satan are laid upon one and the favor of God and the co-inheritance with Christ are taken away. Grace in an infant weakens and stifles sin, but sin can again come to life and grow if it is given food and freedom. And so, the whole attention of those who have the obligation of preserving whole the Christian child who has been received from the font should be directed to not allowing sin in any way to take possession of him again, to crushing sin and making it powerless by every means, and to arousing and strengthening the child's orientation towards God. One must act in such a way that this attitude in the growing Christian will grow by itself, even though under the guidance of someone else, and that he will more and more become accustomed to prevail over sin and conquer it for the sake of pleasing God, and will grow accustomed to exercise his powers of spirit and body in such a way that they will work not for sin but for the service of God.

That this is possible is evident from the fact that the one who has been born and baptized is entirely a seed of the future, or a field filled with seeds. The new attitude poured into him by the grace of baptism is not only something thought or imagined, but is something actual, that is, it is also a seed of life.

If in general every seed is developed according to its kind, then the seed of the grace-given life in the baptized one also can be developed. If there is placed in him the seed of a turning towards God which overcomes sin, then it likewise can be developed and nurtured as other seeds are. But one must use effective means for this, or, in other words, define a consistent means of acting upon the baptized infant.

## THE GOAL OF OUR BAPTISM

The aim towards which everything in this proc- ess should be directed is this: that this new man, when he comes to awareness, might recognize himself not only as a rational and free man, but at the same time as a person who has entered into an obligation with the Lord, with Whom his eternal lot is joined inseparably; and that he might not only acknowledge himself to be such, but might also find himself capable of acting according to this obligation and might see that his pre-eminent attraction is to this.

The question arises, how can this be attained? How should one act with regard to a baptized child so that when he comes to age he might not desire anything else than to be a true Christian? In other words, how does one raise him up in a Christian way?

To answer this we will not undertake to examine everything in detail. We will limit ourselves to a general survey of the whole topic of Christian upbringing, having in mind to show how, in every circumstance, to support and strengthen the good side in children, and how to make powerless and crush what is bad.

Here, first of all, our attention should be directed to the infant in the cradle before any kind of capabilities have awakened in him. The child is alive; consequently one can influence his life. Here we should think of the influence of the Holy Mysteries, and with them the whole churchly way of life, and at the same time the faith and piety of the parents. All this together constitutes a saving atmosphere around the infant. By all of this the life of grace which has been conceived in the infant is instilled mystically.

The frequent Communion of the Holy Mysteries of Christ (one should add, as frequently as possible) joins this new member to the Lord in the most lively and active way through His most pure Body and Blood. It sanctifies him, gives him peace within himself, and makes him inaccessible to the dark powers. People who follow this advice notice that on the day when a child is given Communion, he is immersed in a deep calm without powerful movements of all his natural needs, even those which are most powerfully felt in children. Sometimes the child is filled with joy and a playfulness of spirit in which he is ready to embrace everyone as his own.

Often Holy Communion is accompanied also by miracles. Saint Andrew of Crete in his childhood did not speak for a long time, but when his grieved parents turned to prayer and the reception of grace, during the time of Communion the Lord by His grace loosed the bonds of his tongue, which afterwards gave the Church to drink of torrents of eloquence and wisdom. One doctor, from his own observation, testifies that for the most part when there are illnesses in children the children should be taken to Holy Communion, and very rarely does he have need to use later any kind of medical help.

A great influence is exercised on the child by frequently taking him to Church, by having him kiss the holy Cross, the Gospel, the icons, and by covering him with the veils. Likewise, at home frequently placing him under the icons, frequently signing him with the sign of the Cross, sprinkling him with holy water, the burning of incense, making the sign of the Cross over his cradle, his food, and everything connected with him, the blessing of a priest, the bringing into the house of icons from Church, the service of molebens[1]—and in general everything from the Church, in a wondrous way warms and nourishes the life of grace in the child and is always the most safe and impenetrable protection against the attacks of the invisible dark powers who everywhere are ready to penetrate into the developing soul so as to infect it by their activity.

Behind this visible protection there is an invisible one: the guardian angel placed by the Lord to protect the child from the very minute of his baptism. He watches over him and by his presence invisibly influences him, and when necessary inspires the parents to know what they should for a child who is in danger.

But all these strong protections and these powerful and active

---

[1]  Services of intercession

27

inspirations can be dissolved and made fruitless by unbelief, carelessness, impiety, and the bad life of the parents. This is because the means mentioned here are either not used, or are used not in the proper way; here the inward influence of the parents on the child is especially important. It is true that the Lord is merciful to the innocent; but there is a tie which we cannot understand between the souls of the parents and the soul of the child, and we cannot define the extent of the influence of the former on the latter.

At the same time, when the parents exert a bad influence, to some extent mercy and condescension of God are still given to the child. But it sometimes happens that this divine aid ceases, and then the causes which have been prepared bring forth their fruit. Therefore, the spirit of faith and piety of the parents should be regarded as the most powerful means for the preservation, upbringing, and strengthening of the life of grace in children.

# Chapter Three
# The Developing Child

The spirit of the infant has, as it were, no movement as yet in the first days, months, and even years. It is impossible to communicate anything for him to assimilate by the usual means of communication, but one may influence him in another way.

There is a certain special way of communication between souls through the heart. One spirit influences another by means of the feelings. The ease of exerting such an influence upon the soul of an infant is in direct proportion to the fulness and depth of the parents' feeling for the child.

## THE CENTRALITY OF PARENTS
The father and mother as it were disappear into the child and put their whole soul into his welfare. And if their spirit is penetrated with piety, it cannot be that in some way this will not influence the soul of the child.

The best outward conductor in this respect is the eyes. Whereas in the other senses the soul remains hidden, the eyes open their gaze to others. This is the meeting place of one soul with another. Let the openings be used for the passage of holy feelings from the souls of the mother and father to the soul of the child. Their souls cannot help but anoint the soul of the child with this holy oil.

It is necessary that in the gaze of the parents there should be not only love, which is so natural, but also the faith that in their arms there is something more than a simple child. The parents must have the hope that He Who gave them this treasure under their watch as a vessel of grace might furnish them also with sufficient means to preserve him. Finally, there should be ceaseless prayer performed in the spirit, aroused by hope according to faith.

When in this way the parents protect the cradle of their child with this spirit of sincere piety, and when at the same time, on the one hand the guardian angel, and on the other the Holy Mysteries and all of Church life, act upon him from without and from within—by this there is formed around the newly-begun life a spiritual atmosphere akin to it which will pour into it its own character, just as blood, the principle of animal life, derives many of its characteristics from the surrounding atmosphere.

It is said that a newly-made vessel will preserve for a long time, perhaps permanently, the odor of whatever was poured into it at that time. This can also be said about the atmosphere surrounding children. It penetrates in a grace-giving and saving way into the forms of life just being established in the child and places its seal upon him. Here also there is a protection that cannot be penetrated by the influence of evil spirits.

Having begun in such a way from the cradle, one must continue it later, and during the whole time of upbringing: in childhood, in adoloscence, and in young adulthood. The Church, its life, and the Holy Mysteries are like a tabernacle (tent) for the children, and they should be under it without leaving it.

Examples indicate how saving and fruitful this is (such as the life of the Prophet Samuel; the life of Saint Theodore Sykeote, April 22; and others). These alone can even replace all the means of upbringing, as indeed has been done in many cases successfully. The ancient method of upbringing consisted primarily in precisely this.

When a child's powers begin to awaken, one after another,

parents and those who are raising children should double their attention. For when, under the influence of the means which have been indicated, the longing for God will grow and increase in them and draw the powers of the child after it, at this same time the sin which dwells in them also does not sleep, but strives to take possession of these same powers.

The inevitable consequence of this is inward warfare. Since children are incapable of conducting it themselves, their place is understandably taken by the parents. But since this warfare must be conducted through the powers of the children, the parents must strictly watch over the first beginnings of their awakening, so that from the first minute they may give these powers a direction in harmony with the chief aim towards which they must be directed.

Thus begins the warfare of the parents with the sin that dwells in the child. Although this sin is deprived of points of support, still it acts, and so as to find a good resting place for itself it tries to take possession of the powers of the body and soul. One must not allow it to do this, but must, as it were, uproot these powers from the hand of sin and give them over to God.

But so that this might be done with a good foundation and with a rational knowledge of the reliability of the means that has been chosen, one must make clear for oneself what it is that sin desires, what nourishes it, and precisely how it takes possession of us. The fundamental things which arouse and draw one towards sin are: arbitrariness of mind (or curiosity) in the mental faculty, self-will in the faculty of will, and pleasures in the faculty of feeling.

Therefore one must so conduct and direct the developing powers of the soul and body so as not to give them over into captivity to enjoyments of the flesh, to curiosity, to self-will and self-centered pleasures—for this would be a sinful captivity—but on the contrary, one must train the child how to separate himself from them and master them, and thus as much as possible to render them powerless and harmless. This is the chief thing in the beginning. The whole of the upbringing can later be brought into harmony with this beginning. Let us look again, with this aim, at the chief activities of the body, soul, and spirit.

## PHYSICAL NEEDS

First of all, the needs of the body are aroused and then are in a constant state of living activity until death itself. It is all the more essential to place them within their proper bounds and to strengthen them with the force of habit, so that later there will be less disturbance from them.

### Food

The first requirement for bodily life is food. With relation to morality, this is the seat of the passion for sinful enjoyment of the flesh, or the arena for its development and nourishment. Therefore, one must feed the child in such a way that in developing the life of the body, furnishing him strength and health, one will not ignite in the soul the pleasing of the flesh.

One should not regard that the child is small (and therefore in no need of such concern). From the very first years one must begin to restrain the flesh which is inclined to crude materiality, and train the child to become master of it, so that in adolescence and youth, and in the years thereafter, he might easily and freely be in control of this need.

The first attempt made is very precious. Much that happens subsequently depends on the feeding of the child. Without noticing it, one can develop in him the love of pleasure and immoderation in food—the two forms of the sin of gluttony, the two inclinations bound up with eating that are so ruinous for the body and the soul.

Therefore, even physicians and teachers advise:

1) to select a healthful and suitable food, depending on the age of the child, for one food is suitable for an infant, another for a

child, yet another for an adolescent and a young adult;

2) to subject the use of food to definite rules (again, adapted to age), in which there should be defined the time, the quantity, and the means of eating; and

3) not to depart later from this established rule without need. By these means the child is trained not to demand food always whenever he wants to eat, but to wait for the assigned time; here are to be found the first attempts at exercising oneself in denying oneself one's desires.

When a child is fed every time he cries, and then every time he asks to eat, he is so weakened by this that later he cannot refuse food except with great pain. At the same time, this accustoms him to getting his own will, because he succeeds in getting whatever he asks for or cries for.

Sleep also should be subjected to the same kind of measure, as should warmth and cold, and other comforts which are necessary in one's upbringing, having unfailingly in mind not to ignite the passion for sensual enjoyments, and to train one to deny oneself. This should be strictly observed during the whole time of the upbringing of the child—changing the rules, it goes without saying, in their application (to circumstances and age), but not in essence, until the child, being firmly established in them, will take himself in hand.

*Movement*

The second function of the body is movement. Its organ is the muscles, in which lie the power and strength of the body, the means of labor. With relation to the soul this is the seat of the will, and it very easily develops self-will. The measured and sensible development of this function, giving to the body stimulation and animation, trains one to labor and forms the habit of stability.

On the contrary, an unsteady development, left to the will of the child, develops in some a hyperactivity and inattentiveness, and in others a slowness, lifelessness, and laziness. In the former case, self-will and disobedience are turned into a law, in connection with which are to be found also aggressiveness, anger, and unrestraint in one's desires. In the latter case, one becomes immersed in the flesh and given over to sensual enjoyments.

Therefore, one should have in view that in strengthening the powers of the body one should not thereby inflate self-will and destroy the spirit for the sake of the flesh. To avoid this the chief things are moderation, a definite schedule, and supervision. Let the child play, but let it be in the place and in the way which are indicated to him.

The will of the parents should be imprinted upon each step—of course in a general way. Without this, the behavior of the child can easily become corrupted. After enjoying himself according to his own will, the child always returns unwilling to obey even in the smallest things; and this is if it happens only once—what then can one say if this part of bodily activity is completely neglected? How difficult it is later to uproot self-will, which so quickly seats itself in the body as in a fortress. The neck will not bend, the hands and feet will not move, and the eyes will not even wish to look as they are told.

But on the contrary, a child comes out ready to obey any kind of order when from the very beginning he is not given total freedom in his movements. In addition, there is no better training in being the master of one's body than by forcing it to exert itself according to orders.

### Senses

The third function of the body is the nerves. From the nerves come the senses—the means of observation and food for curiosity; but more of this later. Here we will talk about the general purpose of the nerves as the center of the sensuality of the body, or the capability of receiving outward impressions which are unpleasant for it.

In this respect one must make a rule to train the body to endure every kind of outward influence without misfortune: whether from fresh air, water, change of temperature, heat, cold, pain, wounds, and so forth. Whoever has acquired such a habit is the most fortunate of men, capable of the most difficult actions at any time and in any place. The soul in such a man is the full master of the body; it does not postpone, or change, or leave off actions fearing bodily unpleasantness. On the contrary, it will turn with a certain desire to those things that can bring danger to the body; this is very important.

The chief evil with relation to the body is love for the body and pitying it. This takes away all the soul's authority over the body and makes the soul the slave of the body. And on the contrary, one who does not spare the body will not be disturbed in whatever he does by apprehensions born of blind love of life. How fortunate is one who is trained to this from childhood!

Here also is the place for medical advice concerning bathing, the times and places of walking, and clothing; the chief thing is to keep the body not in such a state that it would receive only pleasant impressions, but on the contrary, to keep it more under the impression of those things which cause it disturbance. By pleasant impressions the body is pampered, and by unpleasant ones it is strengthened; in the former condition the child is afraid of everything, but in the latter condition it is ready for anything and is capable of continuing patiently what it has begun.

Such an attitude toward the body is prescribed by the science of raising children. Here we will only indicate how these counsels are useful also for the development of Christian life—because the zealous fulfillment of them protects the entrance into the soul of the evil poison of sensual enjoyments, of self-will, of love for the body and self-pity; and it forms in the child the dispositions which are opposite to these, and in general trains him to be the master of his body and not to be in submission to it. And this is very important in the Christian life, which by its nature is remote from sensuality and every kind of pleasing of the flesh.

And so we should not leave to arbitrary decision the development of the child's body, but must keep it under a strict discipline from the very beginning, until later it may be given into the hands of the child himself as an organ already adapted to Christian life and not hostile to it.

Those Christian parents who truly love their children should not spare anything, even their own parents' heart, in order to furnish this good thing for their children. For otherwise all the acts following their love and concern will either bear little fruit or be entirely fruitless.

The body is the dwelling place of the passions, and chiefly of the fiercest ones, such as lust and anger. It is also the organ through which the demons penetrate into the soul or come to settle near it. It goes without saying that in this process one must not leave out of sight the influence of church life and everything in it that affects the body, for by this the body itself will be sanctified and the greedy, animal life of the child will be restrained.

We will not discuss all this here, but only indicate the chief tone of the influences upon the body. Life itself will give the details for those who need them. In accordance with this outline one may understand also how to treat the body in all the other seasons of life, for the question is the same in all of us.

Together with the manifestation of bodily needs, the lower capabilities of the soul are also not slow in expressing themselves, in their natural order. The child begins to look more closely at one object or another—at one more, at another less, as if one pleases him more and another less. These are the first beginnings of the exercising of the senses, after which there follows immediately an awakening of the activity of imagination and memory. These capabilities stand at the transition point between the activity of the body and that of the soul, and the two act together, so that what is done by the one is immediately communicated to the other.

Judging by the importance which they have at the present time in our life, how good and salutary it is to sanctify these first beginnings with objects from the realm of faith.

First impressions remain deeply imbedded in the memory. We should remember that the soul appears in the world naked; it grows, becomes rich with inner content, and undertakes various forms of activity only later. The first material, the first food for its formation it receives from outside, from the senses, through imagination. It is self-evident of what nature the first objects of the senses and imagination should be in order not only not to hinder, but even more to aid the Christian life which is just being formed.

It is well known that just as the first food has a significant influence on the temperament of the body, so also the first objects with which the soul occupies itself have a powerful influence on the character of the soul or the tone of its life.

# Chapter Four
# Forming Attitudes

If the prescribed order of action on the body and the lower capabilities is strictly kept, the soul will receive from this a splendid preparation for a truly good attitude. However, this is only a preparation; the attitude itself must be formed by a positive action on all his powers: mind, will, and heart.

## THE MIND

In children the power of thinking is quickly manifested. It comes at the same time as speech and grows together with the development of the latter. Therefore, the formation of the mind must be begun together with words. The chief thing to be kept in mind is that there should be sound concepts and judgments, in accordance with Christian principles, about everything the child encounters or that comes to his attention: what is right and what wrong, what is good and what bad. This is very easy to do by means of ordinary conversations and questions. Parents often speak among themselves; children overhear and almost always assimilate not only the ideas, but even turns of speech and gestures.

Therefore, let parents, when they talk, call things always by their proper names. For example: What is the meaning of the present life, and how does it end? Where does everything come from? What are pleasures? What value do certain customs have?

Let parents talk with their children and explain to them either directly or, best of all, by means of stories. Is it good, for example, to dress well? Is it pleasurable when one receives praise? Or let them ask the children what they think of one thing or another, and then correct their mistakes. In a short time, by this simple means, one may communicate sound principles for judging about things, and these principles will not be erased for a long time, and may remain for life.

In this way worldly thinking and evil, insatiable curiosity are suppressed in their very root. Truth binds the mind to what satisfies it, but worldly thinking does not satisfy and therefore ignites curiousity. One does a great favor to children by saving them from this worldly thinking. And this is still before they take to reading books.

Further, one must on no account give children books with corrupt concepts; their minds will thus be preserved whole, in holy and divine healthiness. It is useless not to try to exercise the child in this way, under the supposition that he is still small. Truth is accessible to everyone. That a small Christian child is wiser than philosophers has been shown by experience. This experience is repeated sometimes today, but in earlier times it was everywhere.

For example, during the period of martyrdom, small children discoursed on Christ the Saviour, on the folly of idol-worship, on the future life, and the like; this was because their mother or father had explained these things to them in simple conversations. These truths had then become close to the heart, which began to treasure them all the way to readiness to die for them.

## THE WILL

A child has many desires. Everything catches his attention, attracts him, and gives birth to desires. Being unable to distinguish good from evil, he desires everything, and he is ready to do everything he desires. A child left to himself becomes untamable and self-willed. Therefore, parents must strictly watch this sprout of the soul's activity.

The simplest means for confining the will within its proper bounds lies in disposing children to do nothing without permission. Let them be eager to run to their parents and ask, "May I do this or that?" They should be persuaded by their own experience and that of others that to fulfill their own desires without asking is dangerous; they should be put in such a frame of mind that they even fear their own will. This disposition will be most fortunate, and at the same time it is the easier one to be imprinted. Since children for the most part do address their questions to adults, realizing their own ignorance and weakness, this state of affairs has only to be elevated and placed as an absolute law for them.

The natural consequence of such an attitude will be total obedience and submission in everything to the will of the parents even against one's own will; a disposition to deny oneself in many things, and the habit or ability to do this; and, the chief thing, the conviction, based on experience, that one should not obey oneself in everything. This is all the more understandable for children from their own experience, because they desire many things, and often those things are harmful to their bodies and souls.

While accustoming a child not to do his own will, one must also train him to do good. For this, let the parents themselves furnish a fine example of good life and acquaint their children with people whose chief concerns are not pleasures and awards, but the salvation of the soul. Children love to imitate. How early they learn to copy a mother or father! Here there occurs something similar to what happens with identically tuned instruments.

At the same time, one must inspire the children themselves to good deeds. At first one must order them to do good deeds, and then guide them into doing them themselves. The most ordinary good deeds in this regard are: almsgiving, compassion, mercifulness, yielding to others, and patience. It is not difficult to train them to do these things. Opportunities for them occur every minute; one has only to use them.

From this training, the will emerges well disposed to various good deeds and in general with a tendency towards the good. And doing good must be taught just like everything else.

## THE HEART

If the mind, will, and lower powers are acting in this way, it goes without saying that the heart also will be disposed to have sound and true feelings and to acquire the habit of enjoying what is truly enjoyable and of having no sympathy whatever to that which, under the guise of pleasure, pours poison into the soul and body. The heart is the capability of tasting and feeling satisfaction.

When man was in union with God, he found delight in divine and sacred things by the grace of God. After his fall he lost this taste and began to thirst for what is sensual. The grace of baptism has removed this, but sensuality is again ready to fill the heart. One must not allow this; one must guard the heart.

The most effective means for the education of true taste in the heart is a church-centered life, in which all children in their upbringing must be unfailingly kept. Sympathy for everything sacred, pleasure in remaining in its midst for the sake of quietness and warmth, separation from what is bright and attractive in worldly vanity—all this cannot better be imprinted in the heart (than by a church-centered life). The church building, church singing, icons—these are the first objects of fine art in content and power.

One should remember that it is in accordance with the taste of one's heart that the future eternal mansion will be given, and that the taste in one's heart there will be the very one that is formed here. It is evident that theaters, shows, and similar things are not suitable for Christians.

A soul that has been calmed and ordered in this way will not, in accordance with its natural disorderliness, hinder the development of the spirit. The spirit develops itself more easily than the soul, and it reveals its power and activity earlier than the soul's.

To the spirit belong: 1) The fear of God (corresponding to the mind); 2) Conscience (corresponding to will); and 3) Prayer (corresponding to feeling). The fear of God gives birth to prayer and makes the conscience clear.

There is no need to direct all this to the other, invisible world. Children already have a predisposition for this, and they assimilate these feelings. Especially is prayer ingrafted very easily and acts not through the tongue, but through the heart. This is why children willingly and without fatigue participate in prayers at home and in the church services and are happy to do so. Therefore, they should not be deprived of this part of their education, but little by little they should be led into this sanctuary of our feelings. The earlier the fear of God will be imprinted and prayer aroused, the more solid will piety be for the rest of one's life.

In some children this spirit has been manifested of itself, even among evident obstacles to its uncovering. This is very natural. The spirit of grace received at baptism, if it has not been quenched by an improper development of body and soul, cannot but give life to our spirit, and what can prevent it from being manifested in its power?

Conscience, however, demands the closest guidance. Sound concepts, together with the good example of the parents and other means of teaching the good, and prayer illuminate the conscience and imprint in it sufficient foundations for subsequent good activity. But the chief thing is that one should form in children an attitude of conscientiousness and awareness. Awareness is something extraordinarily important in life; but however easy it is to form it, it is just as easy to stifle it in children.

The will of the parents for small children is the law of

conscience and of God. Let parents, in accordance with their best understanding, give their commands in such a way that children are not forced to be transgressors of their will; and if they have already become such, they should be disposed as much as possible to repentance.

What frost is for flowers, so is the transgression of the parents' will for a child; he cannot look you in the eyes, he does not desire to enjoy kindnesses, he wishes to run away and be alone; but at the same time his soul becomes crude, and the child begins to grow wild. It is a good thing to dispose him ahead of time to repentance, so that without fear, with trust and with tears, he might come and say, "I did something wrong."

It goes without saying that all this will concern only ordinary things; but what is good is that here a foundation is placed for a future constant and truly religious character—to rise up immediately after a fall—and there is formed the capability of speedy repentance and cleansing or renewing oneself by tears.

We have given here the order of a child's life. Let a child grow in it, and the spirit of piety will develop more in him. The parents should follow all the movements of the child's awakening powers and direct everything to a single end.

This is the rule: begin with the child's very first breath; begin everything at once, and not just one thing; do this all unceasingly, evenly, by degrees, without jumps, with patience and expectation, observing a wise gradualness, taking note of the sprouts and making use of them, considering nothing unimportant in such an important matter. We will not go here into details, for we have in mind to indicate only the chief direction of upbringing.

# Chapter Five
# The Years of Youth

One cannot define just when a person comes to the awareness of himself as being a Christian and to the independent resolve to live in a Christian way. In actual fact this happens at different times: at the age of seven, ten, fifteen, or later. It may be that the time of study comes before this, as usually happens.

## INSTRUCTION

At the same time there is an unchanging rule: one must keep the whole previous order without change during the whole time of study also, for it proceeds essentially from the nature of our capabilities and from the demands of Christian life. The order of study must not be placed in opposition to the indicated outlook, otherwise everything will be destroyed which was created there. That is, one must preserve young students, just like infants, by means of the piety of everything surrounding them, by means of church life and the Mysteries; and likewise one must act upon their body, soul, and spirit.

At the same time, practically speaking, to the teaching itself one must add only this: Let instruction be so arranged that it will be evident what is the main point and what is secondary.

This idea is easiest to imprint through a division of the objects of study and the time for them. Let the study of faith be considered the chief thing. Let the best time be assigned to works of piety, and in case of conflict let them take the first place over learning. Let approval be given not only for success in learning, but likewise for faith and good behavior.

In general, one must so dispose the mind of pupils that they do not lose the conviction that our chief work is the pleasing of God, and that learning is a secondary quality, something incidental, which is good only during the present life. This is why it should not at all be placed so high and in such an attractive form that it will occupy all one's attention and absorb all one's concern.

There is nothing more poisonous or ruinous for the spirit of Christian life than such learning and an exclusive concern for it. It casts one straight into coldness and then can keep one forever in it, and sometimes it also adds to this an immoral life, if there are conditions which are favorable for this.

The second thing to which attention should be given is the spirit of the instruction or of the attitude towards the objects of study. It should be placed as an unfailing law that every kind of learning which is taught to a Christian should be penetrated with Christian principles, and more precisely, Orthodox ones. Every branch of learning is capable of this approach, and it will be a true kind of learning only when this condition is fulfilled.

Christian principles are true beyond doubt. Therefore, without any doubting, make them the general measuring-stick of truth. It is a most dangerous error among us that subjects of learning are taught without any attention to the true faith; one allows oneself freethinking and even lying under the supposition that faith and learning are two spheres which are quite distinct.

On the contrary, we have a single spirit. Our spirit receives learning and is imbued with its principles just as it receives faith and is penetrated by it. How is it then possible that these two spheres should not come into contact here, whether favorable or unfavorable? At the same time, the sphere of truth is one. Therefore, why pound into the head that which is not from this

45

sphere?

If instruction will be conducted in this manner, so that faith together with life in the spirit of faith might dominate in the attention of pupils, both in the manner of studying and in the spirit of instruction, then there is no doubt that the principles placed in childhood not only will be preserved, but will increase, be strengthened, and come to a corresponding maturity. And what a good effect this will have!

If one will put in such order the upbringing of a child from his first years, then little by little the character which his whole life should have will be revealed before him, and he will grow more accustomed to the thought that upon him there lies the obligation given by our God and Saviour to live and act according to His decree, that all other deeds and occupations are lower than this and have a place only for the course of the present life, and that there is another dwelling place, another homeland towards which one must direct all one's thoughts and all one's desires.

In the natural course of the development of one's capabilities, everyone naturally comes to the awareness that he is a man. But if to his nature there is ingrafted the new principle of the grace of Christianity at the very moment when a person's powers and their movements are awakened (in baptism), and if then in all the points of the development of these powers this new principle not only does not yield first place—but on the contrary always prevails and gives as it were the form to everything—then when a man comes to full awareness he will find himself at the same time acting according to Christian principles and will find himself to be a Christian.

And this is the chief aim of a Christian upbringing: that a man as a result of this might say within himself that he is a Christian. And if, when he comes to full awareness of himself he will say, "I am a Christian, obliged by my Saviour and God to live in such a way so as to be vouchsafed the blessed communion with Him and

46

with His chosen ones in the future life," then in the very midst of his independent existence or the unique, rational ordering of his life, he will place for himself as his first and essential duty to preserve in an independent way and to warm the spirit of piety in which he previously walked under the guidance of others.

## THE YOKE OF CHRIST

It has already been noted that there must be a special moment when one must intentionally renew in one's awareness all the obligations of Christianity and place upon oneself their yoke as an unfailing law.

In baptism they were accepted without awareness because then they were kept more by the mind and attitude of someone else and in simplicity, but now one must consciously place upon oneself the good yoke of Christ, choose the life of Christianity, and exclusively dedicate oneself to God, so that later all the days of one's life one might serve Him with enthusiasm. Here only does a man himself begin the Christian life. It existed in him previously also, but one may say it proceeded not from his own activity, not from his own person.

Now he himself, in his own person, begins to act in the spirit of a Christian. Before this, the light of Christ was in him like the light of the first day (of creation), which came not from one central source, but was diffused. But just as centers had to be provided for the light, drawing it to the suns and planets, so also this (spiritual) light must be gathered together around the central point of our life—our consciousness.

A man becomes entirely human when he comes to self-awareness and independence of mind, when he becomes the complete master and commander of his own ideas and deeds and holds certain ideas not because others have given these to him, but because he himself finds them to be true. A man, when he becomes a Christian, still remains a man, and therefore in his

47

Christianity he must also be rational, only this rationality he should turn to the profit of holy faith. Let him become rationally convinced that the holy faith which he confesses is the only faithful path of salvation, and that all other paths which are not in agreement with it lead to perdition. It is no honor to a man to be a blind confessor; he must be a conscious confessor, so that acting in this way, he acts as he should.

All this he does when he consciously places upon himself the good yoke of Christ.

Only here does one's personal faith, or one's good life according to faith, become firm and unshakable. One will not be scandalized by a bad example, will not be attracted by empty thoughts, because he is clearly conscious of the obligation of thinking and acting already in a definite way.

But if he has become conscious of this, then just as previously a good example inclined him to follow it, so now a bad example can dispose him to do what is bad, can draw him to sin. And just as the good thoughts of others previously possessed his mind easily and without protest, so now evil thoughts take possession of him. In experience it is evident how precarious is the confession of faith and goodness of life in a man who previously has not become conscious of himself as a Christian. He who encounters few temptations will continue to mature longer in simplicity of heart; but one who cannot escape them will stand before great danger. We see in the lives of all who have preserved the grace of baptism that there was in these lives a moment when they decisively dedicated themselves to God; this is indicated by such words as "he became inflamed in spirit" or "he was ignited by a divine desire."

Let him who has become conscious of himself as a Christian, or has consciously decided to live in a Christian way, himself now preserve with all care the perfection and purity of life which he has received at a younger age, just as others have preserved this life before him. There is no need to offer special rules as a guide for him. In this respect he is the same as one who is repenting, and having abandoned sin has enthusiastic resoluteness to live in a Christian way. Therefore, from now on he should be guided by the same rules already mentioned above. The difference between this kind of person and one who has repented and is on the way to perfection is already clear without any explanation.

Now we must make several very important warnings which refer exclusively to youth. How good and saving it is not only to be directed in a Christian way in one's upbringing, but also later to acknowledge oneself and decide to be a Christian before entering upon the years of mature youth. This is essential in view of the great dangers to which a youth is inevitably subjected: 1) from the very nature of his age, and 2) from the great temptations which occur throughout youth.

# Chapter Six
## Understanding a Young Person

The river of our life is interrupted by the turbulent period of youth. This is the time when the life of body and spirit is boiling at full steam. A child lives quietly; a mature man has few violent shocks; and those who are adorned with grey hairs are already inclined to repose. It is only youth that is boiling with life.

**THE SHOCK-WAVES OF YOUTH**

One must have a very strong foundation so as to stand firm at this time against the shock-waves of youth. The very disorderliness and impulsiveness of the movements of this age are dangerous.

Now there begin a youth's first movements of his own, the beginning of the awakening of his powers, and they have for him a great fascination. By the power of their influence they crowd out everything that had earlier been placed in the mind and heart of the the youth. What was before becomes for him a dream, a prejudice. Only his present feelings seem true; only they seem to have actuality and significance.

However, if before these powers are awakened the youth has bound himself by the obligation of confessing and living as a Christian, then all the new impulses, being secondary, will be weaker and will give way more easily to the demands of the earlier impulses he felt, because the latter are older, have already been tested and chosen by the heart, and—the chief thing—have been made firm by a vow. A youth absolutely wants always to keep his word.

But what can one say to someone who not only does not love Christian life and truth, but has never even heard of it? In this case he is a house without protection, given over to robbery, or a dry branch given over to burning in a fire. When the arbitrariness of youthful ideas throw a shadow of doubt on everything, when the arousal of the passions are causing a mighty disturbance in him, when the whole soul is filled with tempting thoughts and movements—the young person is in fire.

Who will give him a drop of dew to cool him, or give him a helping hand, if there is not a voice from his own heart that speaks for truth, for goodness, and for purity? But this voice will not come if love for it has not been sown previously. Even good advice in this case will not help; there will be nothing for it to stick to.

Advice and persuasion are powerful if, entering through hearing into the heart, they arouse there feelings which already exist and have a value for us and have only been set aside for the time being, while we simply do not know how to get to them and give them their natural power. In this case advice from someone else is a precious gift to a youth. But if in the heart there are no beginnings of a pure life, such advice is useless.

A youth lives in his own world, and who will investigate all the movements and inclinations of his heart? This is the same thing as investigating the path of a bird in the air, or the course of a ship in the water! The bubbling of a fermenting liquid, the movement of unlike elements when mixed together—this is the heart of a youth. All the demands of so-called nature are in active arousal; each one speaks up and seeks satisfaction. There is present a disorder in our nature, and so the coming together of these voices is like the disorderly cries of a noisy multitude.

51

What will happen to the youth if he has not been trained in advance to put his movements into a certain order and has not placed upon himself the obligation to preserve them in strict subordination to certain higher demands? If these principles have been deeply impressed upon the heart in his upbringing as a child, and then have been consciously accepted as a rule, then all these agitations will proceed as if on the surface, fleetingly, without moving the foundations or shaking the soul.

The state in which we emerge out of the years of youth depends a great deal upon the state in which we enter into them. Water falling from a cliff foams and swirls below, but then it goes its quiet way in various courses. This is an image of youth, into which everyone is thrown as water into a waterfall. From it there come out two kinds of people: some shine with virtue and nobility, while others are darkened by impiety and a corrupt life.

There is also a third kind, a middle class, a mixture of good with evil, which is something like a firebrand that inclines now towards good and now towards evil, or like a broken clock that sometimes runs well but sometimes runs fast or slow.

He who has earlier made himself firm by an obligation has taken shelter, as it were, in a strong ship which allows no water to come into it, or has made a calm channel through a whirl-pool. Without this even a good upbringing will not always save a person. It may be that a young person might not fall into crude vices, but all the same, if he is not concentrated within himself and if his heart is not separated from everything by means of a vow, it will be pulled this way and that by things that attract him, and he will unfailingly come out of the years of youth in a state of coldness, without reaching harbor anywhere.

How saving it is before the years of youth not only to receive a good outlook, but also to make oneself firm with a vow to be a true Christian. Let one who has decided on this fear youth itself, like fire, and therefore let him flee all cases in which youth can easily be let loose and become untamable.

## TWO TENDENCIES

In itself youth is dangerous; but apart from this, there are two tendencies which are characteristic of this age, and from them the impulses of youth are powerfully inflamed and acquire great power and danger. These are: 1) a thirst for impressions, and 2) an inclination to enter into contact with others. Therefore, as a means for avoiding the dangers of this age, one may advise that these tendencies be subjected to rules, lest in place of good they bring evil. The good dispositions which were aroused earlier will remain in all their power if they are not quenched and not hindered.

### 1) The thirst for impressions

The thirst for impressions gives a certain impetuosity, an uninterruptedness, a variety to the activities of a youth. He wishes constantly to test himself, to see everything, to hear everything, to be everywhere.

You can look for him wherever there is a glitter for the eyes, a harmony for the ears, an open space for movement. He wishes to be under an uninterrupted stream of impressions, always new and therefore various. He does not like to to sit home, does not like to stay in one place, does not like to concentrate on only one activity. His element is enjoying himself.

But this is not enough for him. He is not satisfied with an actual testing of himself, but wishes to assimilate and, as it were, transfer what others have felt, how others have acted by themselves or in circumstances similar to his own.

Then he throws himself into books and begins to read. He goes through one book after another, often without even understanding their contents; he is chiefly interested in finding an "effect," no matter what kind of thing it might be or what it might touch on.

Something new, picturesque, sharp—this for him is the best possible recommendation of a book. Here there is revealed and formed an inclination to light reading, which is the same thirst for impressions, only in a different form. But something more is involved here also.

A youth often becomes bored with reality because it somehow binds him from the side: it ties him down and encloses him too much within definite limits, whereas he is seeking a kind of freedom. Thus he often tears himself away from reality and goes off into a world he has created for himself, and there he begins to act in glory.

Fantasy builds for him whole histories, where for the most part the hero is his own person. The youth is only entering into life; before him there is a deceptive, enticing future. In time he will have to take part in it—but what will he be? Can one not draw aside this curtain and take a look? Fantasy, which is very active at this age, does not tarry with its satisfactions. Here day-dreaming manifests itself and develops in such actions.

Day-dreams, light reading, enjoyments—all these, almost one and the same thing in spirit, are offspring of a thirst for impressions, a thirst for what is new and different. And the harm from them is one and the same. There is no better way to starve the good seeds which have been placed before in the heart of a youth than by these means.

A young blossom planted in a place where the wind blows on it from all sides only endures a little and then dries up; grass on which people frequently walk does not grow; a part of the body which is subjected to friction for a long time becomes numb. The same thing happens to the heart and to the good dispositions in it if one is given over to day-dreams or to empty reading or to enjoyments.

If one stands for a long time in the wind, especially a damp wind, and then comes to a quiet place out of the wind, he feels that everything within him is not quite in its place; the same thing happens in the soul that has been amusing itself, in whatever way. When he returns to himself from his state of distraction, the youth finds that everything in his soul has become distorted. The most important thing that has happened is that everything good has been covered by a kind of veil of forgetfulness, and in the first place stand only those deceptive things which have left their impression on him. Consequently, what was before and should always be is no longer present; one's inclinations have changed, and new ones now take the first place.

Why, after returning to it after some kind of distraction, does the soul begin to grow bored? Because it finds itself robbed.

A distracted person has made his soul a highway, along which, through imagination, tempting objects pass by like shadows and tempt the soul to follow them. And then, when one is thus, so to speak, torn away from oneself, the devil secretly approaches, takes away the good seed, and puts a bad one in its place.

Thus the Saviour taught when He explained who it is that takes away the seed sown by the wayside and who it is that sows the tares. It is the enemy of mankind who does both the one and the other.

And so, young person! Do you desire to preserve the purity and innocence of childhood, or the vow of Christian life without reproach? With as much strength and good sense as you have, refrain from amusements, from disorderly reading of tempting books, and from day-dreams.

How good it is to subject oneself in this regard to a strict and even a most strict discipline, and to be, during the whole time of one's youth, under the guidance of others.

Those youths who are not allowed to arrange their own conduct until they reach the age of adulthood, one can call happy. And every youth should rejoice if he is placed in such circumstances. A young person, quite clearly, is scarcely able to come to this by himself; but he shows much sense if he believes the counsel to be more at home at his work, not to day-dream, and not to read empty things. Let him avoid amusements by love of labor, and let him avoid day-dreaming by serious occupations under guidance. Reading especially should be subject to such guidance—both the choice of books and the method of reading.

Let everyone arrange this the best way he can; but it must be done. Passions, doubts, inclinations—all are kindled in precisely this unsteady ferment in the mind of a youth.

## 2. An inclination towards contact with others

The second inclination in a youth, just as dangerous as the first, is the inclination towards contact with others. It is revealed in the need for companionship, friendship, and love. All these, if they are in true order, are good; but it is not the youth himself who should place them in this order.

The age of youth is a time of lively feelings. They are in his heart like the ebb and flow of the tide at the ocean shore. Everything occupies his interest; everything astonishes him. Nature and society have opened their treasures before him.

But feelings do not like to be hidden within themselves, and the youth wishes to share them. Then he has need of a person who might share his feelings, that is, a friend and companion. This need is good and noble, but it can also be dangerous! To the one to whom you entrust your feelings you give a certain authority over yourself.

How careful one must be in the choice of a close friend! You may meet someone who can lead you far, far away from the straight path. It goes without saying that good naturally strives towards good and avoids the evil; there is a certain taste for this in the heart. But again, how often it happens that simplicity of heart is enticed by cunning.

Thus, every young person is rightly advised to be careful in the choice of a friend. It is good not to conclude friendship until the friend has been tested.

It is even better to have as one's first friend one's father, or a person who in many respects takes the place of a father, or a relative who is experienced and good. For one who has resolved to live in a Christian way, the first friend given to him by God is his spiritual father. Converse with him, entrust your secrets to him, ponder what he says, and learn. Under his guidance, with prayer, God will send some other friend also, if it is necessary.

There is not as much danger in friendship, however, as there is in companionship. Rarely do we see real friends, but more often just acquaintances and "friends" in the loose sense. And here how much evil is possible, and how much there really is!

There are certain circles of "friends" with very bad ways of life. Being drawn in with them, you do not notice how you become united with them in spirit, just as you do not notice, when you are in a foul smelling place, how foul you yourself smell. People themselves often lose awareness of the indecency of their own conduct and they quite calmly become crude in it. And even if this awareness is awakened in someone (in such a circle), he doesn't have the strength to get out. Each one is afraid to declare this, expecting that afterwards he will be persecuted with sarcasm, and he says, "So let it be, perhaps it will pass away."

"Evil company corrupts good habits" (I Corinthians 15:33). O Lord, deliver everyone from these depths of Satan! For someone who has decided to labor for the Lord, his only companionship is with those who are pious, who are seeking the Lord; one should avoid others and in all sincerity have no close contact with them, following the example of the saints of God.

## UNDERSTANDING SEXUAL ATTRACTION

The very pinnacle of danger for a youth is contact with the other sex. While in the first temptation, a youth may only stray off the straight path; here, in addition, he loses himself. In its first awakening, this matter is mixed up with the need for what is beautiful, a need which from the time of its awakening compels a youth to seek satisfaction for it.

Meanwhile, what is beautiful little by little begins in his soul to take on a form, because we can find nothing more beautiful than this. The image which has thus been formed is carried about in the head of the youth. From this time on he seems to be seeking what is beautiful, that is, ideal, not earthly, but at the same time he meets with one of the opposite sex and is wounded.

A youth should flee this kind of wounding more than any other, because it is a sickness, and a sickness that is all the more dangerous in that the patient wants to be sick all the way to madness.

How can one avoid this wound? Do not go on the path which leads to being wounded. Here is how this path is described in one work on psychology: it has three turning points.

### 1) The special feeling that he is alone

At first there is awakened in the youth some kind of painful feeling (what it is about and where it comes from, he does not know), which expresses itself in the special feeling that he is alone. This is a feeling of loneliness.

From this feeling there is immediately produced another feeling—a certain pity, tenderness, and attention to oneself. Before this he lived as if not noticing himself. But now he turns to himself, examines himself, and constantly finds that he is not bad, that he is not worse than others, he is a person of some value. He begins to sense his own handsomeness, the pleasantness of the form of his body—in other words, to be pleased with himself.

This is the limit of the first movement of temptation towards himself. From this time on the youth turns to the outward world.

## 2) *The conviction that he must be pleasing to others*

This entrance into the outward world is animated by the conviction that he must be pleasing to others. With this conviction he boldly and as it were victoriously goes out into the arena of activity and, perhaps for the first time, makes for himself a law to be neat, clean, orderly, even elegant. He begins to wander, or to seek companions, seemingly without any definite aim, but in accordance with a secret inclination of his heart, which is seeking something.

At the same time, he tries to show how smart he is, how pleasant he is in contact with others, how kind and attentive he can be, and in general, everything by which he hopes to be liked by others. At the same time he gives free reign to the primary organ of contact with other souls—the eyes.

## 3) *He finds something to ignite his disease*

In such a state a youth is like gun powder placed next to a spark, and soon he finds something to ignite his disease. By a glance of the eyes or by a voice which is especially pleasant, as if struck by an arrow or wounded by a shot, he stands in the beginning as if in ecstasy or turned to stone. Coming to himself from this state and recovering, he finds that his attention and his heart are directed to a certain object and are drawn to it with an unconquerable power.

From this time his heart begins to be eaten up by languor. The youth becomes bored, he is immersed in himself, he is occupied with something important, he seeks as if he has lost something, and everything he does is done for the certain person and as if the person is present. He is like someone who is lost; thoughts of food and sleep don't even occur to him, his usual activities are forgotten, and he comes into a disordered state. Nothing is dear to him.

He is afflicted with a fierce illness which gnaws at his heart, hinders his breathing, dries up the very fountains of life. Such is the gradual course of being wounded!

It goes without saying that a youth should guard himself against falling into this misfortune. Do not go on this path! Banish the signs that precede it—the vague sadness and the feeling of loneliness.

Go directly against it. If you have become sad, do not give yourself over to dreams, but begin to do something serious with your attention, and it will pass. If self pity has been aroused in you, or a feeling of how good you are, hasten to sober yourself up and banish this whim with some kind of strictness and discipline to yourself, especially by making clear a sound idea of the insignificance of whatever comes into your head. A chance or intentional belittlement or humbling in this case would be like water poured on fire.

One must take care to suppress and banish this feeling especially because it is a beginning of movement. If you stop here, you will go no further; you will have neither the desire to be especially pleasing to others, nor the pursuit of showing off fine clothes, nor the desire for constantly going out. If these feelings break through, fight with them.

The best protection in this lies in a strict discipline in everything—in bodily labor, and even more in labor of the mind. Increase your studies, sit at home, do not give yourself over to amusements. If you must go out, then guard your senses, avoid the other sex, and—the chief thing—pray.

## TWO RELATED ATTRIBUTES

Besides these dangers which come from the attributes of youth, there are two more.

First of all, an outlook that exalts to the heavens *rational knowledge*, or one's own understanding. A youth considers it a privilege to place a shade of doubt upon everything, and to set aside everything which does not correspond with the measuring stick of his own understanding. By this alone he cuts off from his heart the whole attitude which comes from faith and the Church and remains alone.

Seeking substitutes for what has been abandoned, he throws himself into theories which are fabricated without any correspondence to divine Truth; he entangles himself in these and banishes from his own mind all the truths of faith.

The disaster is even greater if the occasion for these theories is given in the schools, and if such a spirit is the prevailing one there. People today think to gain possession of the truth, but they only gather together foggy ideas, empty and fantastic and for the most part even contradicting common sense; but these ideas attract the inexperienced and become an idol for a curious youth.

Secondly, there is a *worldly outlook*. Even though it might present itself as something profitable, when this prevails in a youth it is ruinous. It is marked by a life according to the impressions of one's senses, by a condition in which a person remains very little within himself but is almost always outside of himself, whether in fact or in dreams.

With such an outlook one hates the inward life and those who speak about it and live by it. True Christians, for them, are mystics who are confused in their understanding, or are hypocrites.

Their understanding of the truth is hindered by the spirit of the world which is present in the circles of worldly life which a youth is allowed unhindered, and is even advised, to come into contact with. By this contact, the world with all its corrupt concepts and customs is pounded into the receptive soul of a youth who has not been warned ahead of time and has not been prepared to stand against it. He is just forming his outlook on life, and this worldly spirit becomes stamped on him as on wax, and he involuntarily becomes its child. But to be such a child is contrary to being a child of God in Christ Jesus.

And so, here are the dangers for youth from being young! And how difficult it is to resist!

61

But for one who has been raised up well and has decided to dedicate himself to God before the years of youth, this age is not so dangerous. He needs only to endure a little, and then there will come the most pure and blessed repose.

Only keep the vow of pure Christian life during this time also, and afterwards you will live with a certain holy, unshakable firmness. Whoever has gone without danger through the years of youth has, as it were, sailed across a stormy river and, looking back, he blesses God. But someone else, with tears in his eyes, turns back in regret and curses himself. You will never recover what you have lost in your youth. Will one who has fallen ever again attain what is possessed by one who has not fallen?

# Chapter Seven
# Preserving God's Grace

From what has been said up to now, one may easily understand the reason why so few preserve the grace of baptism. Upbringing is the cause of everything, both good and evil.

## WHEN UPBRINGING HAS BEEN WEAK

The reason why the grace of baptism is not preserved is because the order, rules, and laws of an upbringing which is adopted to this end are not kept. The chief causes of this are:

1) *Going away from the Church and its grace-giving means.* This starves the sprout of Christian life, disconnecting it from its sources, and it wilts as a flower wilts when it is placed in a warm place.

2) *Failure to pay heed to one's bodily nature.* People think that the body may be developed in every way without harm for the soul, while actually in the bodily members is the seat of the passions, which develop together with its development, become rooted in and take possession of the soul. Penetrating the bodily members, the passions receive in them a place to settle, or they make out of them a certain unapproachable fortress and thereby secure power for themselves for all the time to come.

3) *A development of the powers of the soul which is undiscriminating and is not directed towards a single aim.* People do not see the aim ahead of them, and so do not see the path to it. From this, despite all the concern for the most contemporary education, people do no more than to puff up in themselves curiosity, self-will, and a thirst for pleasures.

4) *Complete forgetfulness of the spirit.* Prayer, fear of God, and conscience are seldom taken into consideration. If there is outward good order, the most inward side of life is always taken for granted and therefore always left to take care of itself. During this time, the most important thing is covered over by secondary things, and the one thing needed is over-shadowed by a multitude of others.

5) *Finally, an exclusive concern for learning and giving oneself over to the world by means of fashionable ideas, rules, and customs.* These are never favorable to the life of grace, but always arm themselves hostilely against it and strive to smother it. How does this happen? When one enters into the age of youth without first putting in place good principles and the determiniation to live in a Christian way. And further, when one does not restrain the attractions of youthful life in a proper order, but gives oneself over to all the thirst for impressions, through amusements, light reading, the heating of the imagination by fantasies, indiscriminate contact with those who are like oneself, and especially with the opposite sex.

Each one of these causes, and even one of them, is sufficient to quench in a young person the life of grace. But it happens for the most part that they act together, and one unfailingly draws another in its wake; and they all together so obstruct the spiritual life that sometimes not even the slightest trace of it can be noticed. It is  as if a man has no spirit at all and was created not for communion with God, does not have the powers fore-ordained for this, and has not received the grace which gives him life.

The reason why a consistent order of upbringing is not kept is to be found either in ignorance of this order or carelessness with regard to it. Upbringing which is left to itself without attention of necessity will take a direction which is corrupt, false, and harmful, at first in the way of life at home and then during the time of study.

But even where, to all appearances, the upbringing is not left without attention and is subjected to the well-known rules, it turns out frequently to be fruitless and deviates from the aim by reason of the false ideas and principles upon which its order is built. The proper thing is not kept in sight and made the chief thing: not the pleasing of God, not the salvation of the soul, but something entirely different—either the development of purely natural powers, or adaptation to an official position, or making oneself suitable for life in the world. But when the beginning is impure and false, then of necessity that which is built upon it cannot lead to good.

## DEVIATIONS FROM A PROPER UPBRINGING

As the chief deviations from a proper upbringing one may indicate:

1) *The putting aside of the means of receiving grace.* This is a natural consequence of forgetting the fact that the person who is being brought up is a Christian and has not only natural, but also grace-given powers. But without these the Christian is a defenseless garden which is trampled by the roaring demons and broken by the storm of sin and the world, with no one and nothing to bring him to his senses and chase them away.

2) *Because preparation is made primarily for happiness in*

*temporal life*, while the memory of eternal life is drowned out. This is what is spoken about at home, commented on in classes, and is the chief subject in simple conversations.

3) *The prevalence of outwardness, superficiality, in everything*, not excluding even the priestly ministry.

Not being prepared at home, and having gone through such an upbringing, a person will unfailingly be confused in his mind, and will look at everything in an improper way. He will see everything in a distorted way, through broken or false spectacles. And therefore he does not even want to hear about the final truth of his aim in life or the means to it. All of this for him is a secondary matter, not to be taken seriously.

## CORRECTING THE COURSE

After this it is not difficult to define what precisely is necessary in order to correct such a bad order of things. One must:

*1) Understand well and assimilate the principles of true Christian upbringing and act according to them, first of all at home.* The upbringing in the home is the root and foundation of everything that follows. One who is well brought up and directed at home will not so easily be knocked off the straight path by a wrong teaching at school.

*2) Immediately after this, one must rebuild on new, true principles the school education*, introduce into it Christian elements, correct what needs correction; and the chief thing: one must at all times keep the education of the child under the most abundant influence of the Holy Church, which by the whole order of its life acts in a saving way upon the formation of the spirit. This would give no opportunity for sinful impulses to blaze up, would weaken the spirit of the world, and would banish the spirit out of the abyss. At the same time one must direct everything from what is temporal to what is eternal, from the outward to the inward, to raise up children of the Church, members of the Kingdom of Heaven.

*3) Most needful of all, one must educate the educators* under the guidance of such persons who know the true education, not in theory, but in practice. Being formed under the supervision of the most experienced educators, they again will hand on their art to others who follow, and so forth.

The educator should go through all the degrees of Christian perfection in order later to know how to behave in the midst of action, to be capable of noticing which way the students are going, and then to act upon them with patience, successfully, powerfully, and fruitfully. This should be a group of the most pure, God-chosen, and holy people. Of all holy works, the education of children is the most holy.

## THE FRUIT OF GODLINESS

The fruit of a good upbringing is the preservation of the grace of holy baptism. This preservation rewards with great abundance all the labors of upbringing. For certain high advantages belong to the person who has preserved the grace of baptism and from his earliest years has dedicated himself to God.

### Wholeness

The first advantage and as it were the foundation of all other advantages is the wholeness of all that is given by nature and grace. A Christian is meant to be a container of extraordinarily exalted powers which are ready to be poured out upon him from the source of all good things, if only he will not put himself into disorder. One who repents, it is true, can also be healed completely; but it would seem that it is not given to him to know and to feel as one who has not fallen; he cannot take delight in that wholeness and possess the boldness that is the result of it.

## Liveliness

From this there follow naturally a liveliness, a lightness, a spontaneous doing of good. One walks in the good as in a world which is the only one akin to him. One who is repenting must for a long time force himself and train himself so as to do good, so as to perform it easily; and even after attaining this, he must constantly keep himself in a state of tension and fear. On the other hand, one who has not fallen lives in simplicity of heart, in a kind of assurance of salvation which blesses him and and is not deceived.

## Evenness

Then in his life there is formed a certain evenness and uninterruptedness. There are neither sudden impulses nor weakenings in him, and just as the breathing occurs in us for the most part evenly, so in him walking in good occurs in the same way. This can happen also in someone who has repented, but it is not acquired quickly, and is not manifested in such perfection. A wheel that has been repaired frequently lets its defects be known, and a clock that has been repaired is not quite as accurate as one that is new and has not been repaired.

## Joyfulness

A person who has not fallen is always young. In the features of his moral character there are reflected the feelings of a child which has not yet become guilty before his father. Here the first feeling of innocence is a childishness in Christ, a kind of ignorance of evil. How much this cuts off unnecessary thoughts and the oppressive agitations of the heart!

Then there is an extraordinary joy, sincere kindness, a quietness of manner. In all power there is revealed in him the fruits of the Spirit indicated by the Apostle: love, joy, peace, long-suffering, kindness, goodness, faithfulness, gentleness, self control (Galatians 5:22-23). He is, as it were, clothed in the bowels of mercy, kindness, humbleness of mind, meekness, longsuffering (Colossians 3:12).

Then he preserves a non-hypocritical joyfulness of manner or a spiritual joy; for in him is the Kingdom of God, which is peace and joy in the Holy Spirit.

Further, characteristic of him is a certain clairvoyance and wisdom which sees everything within himself and around himself and is able to make good use of himself and his deeds. His heart takes on such an attitude that it immediately says to him what he should do and how he should do it.

Finally, one may say that it is characteristic of him not to be afraid of falling, to have a feeling of safety in God. "Who shall separate us from the love of Christ?" (Romans 8:35).

All this together makes him worthy of respect and love. He involuntarily attracts people to himself. The existence of such persons in the world is a great grace of God. They take the place of the nets of the Apostles.

Just as a multitude of iron filings gather together around a powerful magnet, or as a powerful character attracts the weak, so does the power of the Spirit which dwells in him draw to itself everyone, and especially those in whom there are the first stirrings of the Spirit.

## Unshakability

But the chief form of moral perfection which belongs to one who has preserved himself whole in the years of youth is a certain unshakability in virtue for his whole life.

Samuel remained firm in the presence of all the temptations that scandalized in the house of Eli and in the midst of the agitations of the people in society. Joseph in the midst of his evil brothers, in the house of Potiphar, in prison and in glory, equally preserved his soul inviolate.

In truth, "It is good for a man to bear the yoke in his youth" (Lamentations 3:27). "My son, from your youth up choose instruction, and until you are old you will keep finding wisdom .... For in her service you will toil a little while, and soon you will eat of her produce" (Sirach 6:18, 19).

A right outlook is converted, as it were, into nature, and if sometimes it is a little violated, soon it returns to its original state. Therefore in the lives of saints we find for the most part those who have preserved their moral purity and the grace of baptism in youth.

## DEDICATION TO CHRIST OUR GOD

Above all this, one who has preserved purity and dedicated himself to God from his early years does that which is most pleasing to God. He offers to God the most pleasing sacrifice because God is pleased most of all by what is offered first: the first fruits, the firstborn of men and animals, and therefore also by the first years of youth.

An immaculate youth is a pure sacrifice. This is what is chiefly demanded of every sacrifice. This is accomplished by means of overcoming quite a few obstacles, both within ourself and outside, by renouncing pleasures for which, especially at this age, there is a great inclination.

One must dedicate oneself to God, for in this alone is salvation. There is no better and more hopeful time for this than the first movement when we have become aware of ourselves—for who knows what will be tomorrow?

But if someone hopes to live longer without dedicating this time to God, he will only make it difficult for himself, becoming used to a way of life which is opposed to this. And God knows whether or not he will be able to conquer himself later.

And even if he does conquer himself later, what kind of sacrifice is this to God—an offering that is sick, worn out, injured in his members, not whole? Moreover, although this does happen, it is so rare! How rarely does one who has lost innocence succeed in regaining it!

How difficult it is to be converted for someone who has not known a good life from childhood is depicted vividly, from his own experience, by blessed Augustine in his *Confessions*. He says: "The years of boyhood I spent in games and pranks, even those which are not allowed, in disobedience and lack of attention to my parents. When I entered upon youth I began to lead an immoral life, and in three years I became so corrupt that afterwards for the course of twelve years I was constantly intending to correct myself and did not find the strength to do it.

"Even after I had made a turn-around to a decisive breaking of the will, I still tarried for two years, putting off my conversion from day to day. So weak does the will become from the first passions! But even after my decisive conversion and the reception of grace in holy baptism, what I had to endure fighting with my own passions, which drew me powerfully onto the path I had gone on before!"

Is it remarkable that there are so few who are being saved among those who have led a bad youth? This example more clearly than anything else indicates in what great danger is a person who has not received good rules in his youth and has not beforehand dedicated himself to God.

What good fortune therefore it is to receive a good, truly Christian upbringing, to enter with it into the years of youth, and then in the same spirit to enter into the years of adulthood.